Updated Gout CookBook Series (Desserts)

Discover A New 20+ Gout friendly Desserts

For Reversing And Healing Gouty Arthritis

Mary J. Hart

Table Of Content

Berry Chia Pudding

Ingredients :

- 1 cup blended new berries (like strawberries, blueberries, and raspberries)
- 1/4 cup chia seeds
- 1 1/2 cups unsweetened almond milk (or some other plant-based milk)
- 1-2 tablespoons normal sugar of your decision (stevia, agave syrup, or honey)
- Discretionary garnishes: cut almonds, coconut pieces, or extra new berries

Instructions :

1. Blend half of the mixed berries in a blender or food processor until

smooth. The remaining whole berries should be saved for later.

2. Combine the blended berries, chia seeds, almond milk, and the desired amount of natural sweetener in a glass bowl or jar. Blend well to guarantee the chia seeds are uniformly dispersed.

3. Give the mixture another stir after letting it sit for five minutes to prevent clumping.

4. Allow the chia seeds to absorb the liquid and form a pudding-like consistency by covering the bowl or jar and placing it in the refrigerator for at least two hours or overnight.

5. Give the chia pudding a good stir after it has set to break up any clumps and evenly distribute the berries.

6. Serve the berry chia pudding in individual dishes or glasses.

7. Slicing almonds, coconut flakes, or additional fresh berries can be added as desired on top of the reserved whole berries.

8. Enjoy your delicious berry chia pudding, which is good for gout!

9. Planning time: Dessert in about ten minutes

Cinnamon-Grilled Pineapple

Ingredients:

- 1 medium-sized, ripe pineapple
- 1 teaspoon ground cinnamon honey or maple syrup for showering

Directions:

1. Set the grill's temperature to medium.
2. After carefully slicing off the top and bottom of the pineapple, remove the skin.
3. The pineapple can be cut into rings or spears however you like.
4. Sprinkle ground cinnamon equitably over the pineapple cuts, trying to cover the two sides.
5. Grill the pineapple slices for two to three minutes on each side, or until

grill marks appear and the pineapple is slightly caramelized, if desired.

6. Eliminate the barbecued pineapple from the barbecue and move to a serving plate.

7. Optional: Sprinkle a limited quantity of honey or maple syrup over the barbecued pineapple for added pleasantness.

8. The grilled pineapple can be served warm as a delicious dessert that is good for gout.

9. Planning time: About fifteen minutes

Watermelon Granita

Instructions:

- 1 little seedless watermelon
- 1 tablespoon new lemon juice

Instructions: for garnishing with mint leaves:

1. Scoop the flesh out of the watermelon by cutting it in half. Get rid of any seeds.
2. In a blender or food processor, chop the watermelon flesh into chunks.
3. Add the new lemon juice to the blender.
4. The watermelon chunks should be blended until well-combined and smooth.

5. The watermelon mixture should be spread out in a shallow dish or baking pan.
6. Place the dish in the cooler and let it freeze for around 60 minutes.
7. Take the dish out of the freezer one hour later and break the partially frozen watermelon mixture into icy flakes with a fork.
8. Return the dish to the cooler and rehash the scratching system at regular intervals to 1 hour for around 3-4 times, or until the whole combination is changed into granita-like surface.
9. Remove the watermelon mixture from the freezer when it has reached the desired consistency.

10. The watermelon granita can be served in bowls or glasses with mint leaves added if desired.

11. Partake in the reviving and gout-accommodating watermelon granita!

12. Planning time: Around 10 minutes

13. Freezing time: Dessert: About 3 to 4 hours, including scraping intervals

Almond Flour Pancakes:

Ingredients

- 1 cup almond flour,
- 2 tablespoons coconut flour,
- 1/2 teaspoon baking powder,
- a pinch of salt, two large eggs, 1/4 cup unsweetened almond milk (or any other plant-based milk),
- 1 tablespoon melted coconut oil, or any other cooking oil,
- 1 teaspoon vanilla extract.
- Greek yogurt, fresh fruit, and honey drizzled on top

Instructions :

1. In a blending bowl, whisk together the almond flour, coconut flour, baking powder, and salt.

2. Beat the eggs in another bowl. Add the vanilla extract, melted coconut oil, and almond milk. Race until all around consolidated.

3. Combine the dry ingredients with the wet ingredients in a bowl. Stir until a batter forms that is smooth. You can thin the batter out by adding a little more almond milk if it appears to be too thick.

4. Allow the hitter to rest for around 5 minutes to permit the flours to retain the fluid.

5. Heat a non-stick skillet or iron over medium intensity. Gently oil the surface with coconut oil or cooking shower.

6. Pour around 1/4 cup of player onto the skillet for every flapjack. Spread the

batter into a round shape with the back of a spoon.

7. On one side, cook the pancakes for 2 to 3 minutes until bubbles appear on the surface. Flip and cook for another 1-2 minutes on the opposite side, until brilliant brown.

8. Move the cooked flapjacks to a plate and go on with the excess player, lubing the skillet depending on the situation.

9. With fresh fruit, a dollop of Greek yogurt, and honey, if desired, top the almond flour pancakes.

10.   Enjoy your delicious almond flour pancakes, which are good for gout!

11. Planning time: Around 20 minutes

Baked Apples

Ingredients:

- 4 medium-sized apples (like Granny Smith or Honeycrisp)
- 1/4 cup hacked nuts (like pecans or almonds)
- 1 teaspoon ground cinnamon
- 1 tablespoon honey or maple syrup (discretionary)

Directions:

1. Set the oven temperature to 375°F (190°C).
2. Wash the apples completely and wipe them off. Using a spoon or melon baller, remove the core and seeds from each apple, leaving a hollow space.
3. Combine the ground cinnamon and chopped nuts in a small bowl.

4. Fill the cavity of each apple completely with the nut and cinnamon mixture.
5. Place the stuffed apples in a baking dish, and whenever wanted, shower honey or maple syrup over every apple for added pleasantness.
6. Bake for 25 to 30 minutes, covered with foil, in the preheated oven, or until the apples can be easily pierced with a fork.
7. Bake an additional 5 minutes after removing the foil to lightly brown the apples' tops.
8. Before serving, carefully remove the baked apples from the oven and allow them to cool for a few minutes.
9. Serve the prepared apples warm as a tasty and gout-accommodating sweet.

10. Planning time: Baking time of about ten minutes: 30-35 minutes

Coconut Macaroons

Instructions :

1. 2 cups shredded coconut that has not been sweetened, 1/2 cup almond flour, 1/2 cup coconut cream, 1/4 cup honey or maple syrup, 1 teaspoon vanilla extract, and a pinch of salt

2.

3. Pre-heat the oven to 165°C (325°F). Use parchment paper to line a baking sheet.

4. In a blending bowl, join the destroyed coconut, almond flour, coconut cream, honey or maple syrup, vanilla concentrate, and a spot of salt. Make

sure to thoroughly mix everything together.

5. Allow the coconut to absorb the moisture by letting the mixture sit for about five minutes.

6. Use a cookie scoop or tablespoon to portion the mixture onto the prepared baking sheet, forming mounds or using a macaroon mold if desired, once the mixture has slightly hardened.

7. The coconut macaroons should be baked for 15-20 minutes in a preheated oven, or until the edges are golden brown.

8. The macaroons should cool completely on a wire rack after the baking sheet has been taken out of the oven.

9. The macaroons should be carefully removed from the parchment paper and placed on a serving plate once they have cooled.
10. Partake in the brilliant and gout-accommodating coconut macaroons as a sweet treat!
11. Planning time: Baking time of approximately 15 minutes: 20 to 30 minutes

Mango Sorbet

Ingredients:

- 3 ready mangoes
- 1 tablespoon new lemon or lime juice
- 2-3 tablespoons honey or agave syrup (discretionary, change in accordance with taste)
- 1/4 cup water (if necessary)

1. **Instructi**the mangoes and from the pit. Slice the flesh of the mango into chunks.
2. Put the mango chunks in a food processor or blender.
3. Blend the fresh lemon juice or lime juice.
4. Whenever wanted, add honey or agave syrup to improve the sorbet. Start with

two tablespoons and add more or less depending on how you like it.

5. Mix the blend until smooth. Add a small amount of water—about 1/4 cup—if the mixture is too thick to blend properly.

6. Taste the mixture and add more honey, lemon/lime juice, or water to adjust the sweetness or acidity if necessary.

7. Place the mango mixture in a shallow baking dish or pan.

8. Cover the dish and spot it in the cooler for around 4-6 hours, or until the sorbet is firm.

9. Take the dish out of the freezer every hour for the first three hours and scrape and fluff the sorbet mixture

with a fork to break up any ice crystals that may have formed.

10. Let the sorbet freeze for another one to two hours until it is completely set after the final scraping.

11. Scoop the sorbet into bowls or cones when it's ready, and serve as a gout-friendly dessert right away.

12. Planning time: Freezing time of approximately 15 minutes:

Dim Chocolate-Plunged Strawberri

Ingredients :

- 1 pint washed and dried fresh strawberries
- 1 cup dark chocolate chips or chopped dark chocolate (70 percent cocoa or higher)

Instructions:

1. Line a baking sheet or plate with material paper.
2. Melt the dark chocolate chips or chopped dark chocolate in 30-second intervals, stirring in between, in a microwave-safe bowl until completely smooth. Alternately, you can melt the chocolate on the stovetop in a double boiler.

3. Holding every strawberry by the stem, plunge it into the dissolved chocolate, covering it around 3/4 of the way up. Allow any chocolate left over to return to the bowl.
4. Ensure that the chocolate-dipped strawberries do not touch one another before placing them on the baking sheet that has been prepared.
5. Rehash the plunging system with the excess strawberries until all are covered.
6. While the chocolate is still wet, you can sprinkle chopped nuts, coconut flakes, or a pinch of sea salt on top of the chocolate-dipped strawberries if you so choose.

7. Place the baking sheet in the fridge for around 15-20 minutes, or until the chocolate is firm and set.
8. Remove the after the chocolate has set.
9.
10.
11. Transfer the strawberries to a serving plate from the refrigerator.
12. Dark chocolate-dipped strawberries make an elegant and delicious dessert that is good for gout.
13. Time for preparation: Dessert: About 20 minutes, plus time to chill

Date Pistachio Balls

Ingredients:

1. 1 cup pitted dates,
2. 1 cup shelled pistachios,
3. 1 tablespoon unsweetened cocoa powder,
4. 1 teaspoon vanilla extract, and a pinch of salt are all you need. coconut shredded for coating.

Instructions:

- In a food processor, pulse the pistachios until they are finely ground. Be mindful so as not to over-deal with them into a glue.
- With the ground pistachios, add the pitted dates, cocoa powder, vanilla extract, a pinch of salt, and the food processor.

- Process the blend until it frames a tacky mixture that keeps intact when squeezed between your fingers.
- If the mixture appears to be too dry, add a teaspoon of water at a time and pulse until the desired consistency is reached.
- When the batter is prepared, scoop out little divides and roll them into balls utilizing your hands.
- Optional: Roll the pistachio date balls in destroyed coconut to cover them, whenever wanted.
- Place the pistachio date balls on a parchment-lined baking sheet or plate.
- The pistachio date balls should be refrigerated for at least 30 minutes to firm up.

- Subsequent to cooling, the pistachio date balls are fit to be filled in as a flavorful and nutritious gout-accommodating pastry.
- Planning time: About 20 minutes of chilling time: 30 minutes

Blueberry Quinoa Pudding

Ingredients:

- 1 cup cooked quinoa,
- 1/2 cup unsweetened almond milk (or any other plant-based milk),
- 1/4 cup honey or maple syrup,
- 1 teaspoon vanilla extract,
- 1/2 teaspoon ground cinnamon, and 1 cup fresh blueberries

Instructions :

1. In a pot, join the cooked quinoa, almond milk, honey or maple syrup, vanilla concentrate, and ground cinnamon.
2. Place the pan over medium intensity and carry the combination to a stew, blending once in a while.

3. The quinoa mixture should simmer gently for about 15 to 20 minutes, or until it becomes pudding-like in consistency. Reduce the heat to low.

4. Add the fresh blueberries and stir in; cook for another 2 to 3 minutes to allow the blueberries to slightly soften.

5. Eliminate the pan from the intensity and let the quinoa pudding cool for a couple of moments.

6. Divide the quinoa pudding into glasses or serving bowls.

7. For added flavor, you can drizzle honey or a little more ground cinnamon on top if you so choose.

8. As a novel and gout-friendly dessert option, serve the quinoa pudding warm or chilled.

9. Time for preparation: 25mins

Avocado Chocolate Mousse

Instructions:

- 2 ready avocados
- 1/4 cup unsweetened cocoa powder
- 1/4 cup honey or maple syrup
- 1 teaspoon vanilla concentrate
- Spot of salt
- Discretionary garnishes: shaved dark chocolate, chopped nuts, or sliced strawberries

Instructions:

1. Slice the avocados down the middle, eliminate the pits, and scoop the tissue into a blender or food processor.
2. The avocado should be blended with the cocoa powder, honey or maple syrup, vanilla extract, and a pinch of salt.

3. Scraping the sides of the blender as needed, blend the mixture until smooth and creamy.

4. Taste the chocolate mousse and, if you like, add more honey/maple syrup or cocoa powder to adjust the sweetness or flavor of the cocoa.

5. Transfer the avocado chocolate mousse to serving dishes or ramekins when the desired consistency and flavor have been achieved.

6. For added texture and presentation, you can top the mousse with sliced strawberries, chopped nuts, or shaved dark chocolate if you so choose.

7. To chill and set, place the avocado chocolate mousse in the refrigerator for at least one hour.

8. The avocado chocolate mousse is ready to serve as a gout-friendly dessert after being chilled.
9. Time for preparation: Dessert in about ten minutes

Chia Pudding Parfait

Ingredient :
- 1 cup unsweetened almond milk (or any other plant-based milk) 1/4 cup chopped nuts (such as almonds or walnuts)
- 1 cup mixed berries (such as strawberries, blueberries, and raspberries)
- 1 tablespoon honey or maple syrup
- 1 teaspoon vanilla extract toppings made of granola or shredded coconut:

Instructions :
1. In a bowl, join the chia seeds, almond milk, honey or maple syrup, and vanilla concentrate.

2. Mix the combination well to equally circulate the chia seeds. Allow it to sit for around 5 minutes.

3. Following 5 minutes, give the blend one more great mix to forestall bunching of the chia seeds.

4. Cover the bowl and refrigerate it for no less than 2 hours, or short-term, to permit the chia seeds to retain the fluid and thicken into a pudding-like consistency.

5. Remove the chia pudding from the refrigerator once it has set.

6. To resemble a parfait, arrange the chia pudding and mixed berries in serving bowls or glasses.

7. Keep layering until all of the glasses or bowls are full.

8. Top the chia pudding parfait with cleaved nuts and any extra fixings you want, like destroyed coconut or granola.

9. Serve the chia pudding parfait right away, or refrigerate for a brief time longer in the event that you lean toward it chilled.

10. Planning time: Dessert in about ten minutes

Banana Ice Cream Bites

Ingredients:

- 2 ripe bananas,
- 1/4 cup unsweetened almond butter (or any other nut butter),
- 2 tablespoons chopped dark chocolate (70 percent cocoa or higher),
- 2 tablespoons unsweetened cocoa powder. either freeze-dried fruit, crushed nuts, or shredded coconut

Instructions :

1. Strip the bananas and cut them into meager rounds.
2. Place half of the banana slices on a parchment-lined baking sheet.
3. Melt the almond butter in a small microwave-safe bowl until it is smooth

and pourable. This can be done with stirring in between short intervals.

4. On the baking sheet, drizzle a small amount of melted almond butter over each banana slice.

5. Sprinkle the cocoa powder and cleaved dim chocolate over the banana cuts.

6. Put one more banana cut on top of each covered cut to make a sandwich.

7. Optional: For added flavor and texture, you can roll the edges of the banana sandwiches in crushed freeze-dried fruit, shredded coconut, or nuts.

8. To hold each banana sandwich together, poke a toothpick or small skewer through the middle.

9. Place the baking sheet with the banana frozen yogurt chomps in the

cooler for no less than 2 hours, or until they are frozen strong.

10.   Once frozen, eliminate the banana frozen yogurt chomps from the baking sheet and move them to an impermeable holder or cooler pack for capacity.

11. The banana ice cream bites are a delicious and gout-friendly frozen treat that can be served right out of the freezer.

12. Time for preparation: About fifteen minutes

Pizza with Watermelon

Ingredients:

- 1 little watermelon, cut into round plates
- 1 cup Greek yogurt or coconut yogurt
- 1 cup blended berries (like strawberries, blueberries, and raspberries)
- 1/4 cup cut almonds or slashed pistachios
- New mint leaves for decorate

Instruction :

1. Cut the watermelon into round plates, roughly 1 inch thick, to look like pizza hulls.
2. The watermelon discs should be placed on individual plates or a serving platter.

3. On each watermelon disc, use a generous layer of Greek yogurt or coconut yogurt to cover it like pizza sauce.

4. Organize the blended berries on top of the yogurt, very much like pizza fixings.

5. For a delicious crunch, sprinkle the berries with chopped pistachios or almonds.

6. Fresh mint leaves can be used as a garnish on the watermelon pizza for extra freshness and presentation.

7. Serve the watermelon pizza right away and partake in the reviving and gout-accommodating sweet.

8. Time for preparation: Dessert in about ten minutes:

Raspberry Chia Jam Bars

Ingredients :

- 2 cups raspberries, fresh or frozen, 2 tablespoons chia seeds, 1 to 2 tablespoons honey or maple syrup (adjust to taste)
- 1 1/2 cups almond flour
- 1/4 cup coconut flour
- 1/4 cup dissolved coconut oil
- 2 tablespoons honey or maple syrup
- 1 teaspoon vanilla concentrate
- Touch of salt

Directions:

1. Prepare a square baking dish by lining it with parchment paper and preheating the oven to 350°F (175°C).
2. For the jam, combine the raspberries with honey or maple syrup in a small

saucepan. Mash the berries with a fork or spoon over medium heat.

3. Carry the combination to a stew and let it cook for around 5 minutes, mixing infrequently.

4. Stir in the chia seeds after taking the pan off the heat. Permit the blend to cool for around 10 minutes, during which the chia seeds will thicken the jam.

5. Almond flour, coconut flour, salt, melted coconut oil, honey or maple syrup, vanilla extract, and honey or maple syrup should all be combined in a separate bowl. Combine all ingredients together until a crumbly dough forms.

6. Press 66% of the mixture equally into the lower part of the pre-arranged baking dish to frame the hull.
7. Over the crust, distribute the raspberry chia jam evenly.
8. To create the topping, crumble the remaining dough over the jam layer.
9. Bake for 25 to 30 minutes, or until the edges are golden brown, in an oven that has been preheated.
10. Allow the bars to cool completely in the baking dish after taking them out of the oven.
11. Once cooled, cautiously lift the bars out of the dish utilizing the material paper and move them to a cutting board.

12. Enjoy the delicious and gout-friendly raspberry chia jam bars by slicing them into bars of your choice!
13. Time for preparation: About thirty minutes

Pistachio Rosewater Semolina Cake

Ingredients:

For the Cake:

- 1 cup semolina flour
- 1/2 cup almond flour
- 1/2 cup pistachios, finely ground
- 1/2 cup honey or maple syrup
- 1/2 cup plain yogurt
- 1/4 cup melted butter or coconut oil
- 2 eggs
- 1 teaspoon baking powder
- 1 teaspoon rosewater
- 1/2 teaspoon vanilla extract
- Pinch of salt
- For the Rosewater Syrup:
- 1/4 cup honey or maple syrup

- 1/4 cup water
- 1 tablespoon rosewater

For Garnish:

- Crushed pistachios
- Edible rose petals (optional)

Instructions:

1. Preheat your oven to 350°F (175°C) and grease a round cake pan.
2. In a large bowl, combine the semolina flour, almond flour, ground pistachios, baking powder, and salt.
3. In a separate bowl, whisk together the honey or maple syrup, plain yogurt, melted butter or coconut oil, eggs, rosewater, and vanilla extract until well combined.
4. Pour the wet ingredients into the dry ingredients and mix until a smooth batter forms.

5. Pour the batter into the greased cake pan and spread it out evenly.

6. Bake in the preheated oven for 25-30 minutes, or until a toothpick inserted into the center comes out clean.

7. While the cake is baking, prepare the rosewater syrup. In a small saucepan, combine the honey or maple syrup, water, and rosewater. Heat over low heat until the mixture is well combined and slightly thickened.

8. Once the cake is baked, remove it from the oven and let it cool in the pan for a few minutes.

9. While the cake is still warm, poke several holes on the top using a skewer or fork.

10. Slowly pour the rosewater syrup over the warm cake, allowing it to seep into the holes.

11. Let the cake cool completely in the pan.

12. Once cooled, carefully remove the cake from the pan and transfer it to a serving plate.

13. Garnish the pistachio rosewater semolina cake with crushed pistachios and edible rose petals, if desired.

14. Slice and serve the gout-friendly pistachio rosewater semolina cake for a fragrant and delightful dessert.

15. Preparation time: Approximately 30 minutes

16. Baking time: 25-30 minutes

Chia Seed Pudding Parfait

Ingredients :

For the Chia Seed Cake:

- For the Parfait Layers
- 1/4 cup chia seeds,
- 1 cup almond milk, or any other plant-based milk,
- 2 tablespoons honey, maple syrup, or vanilla extract.
- 1 cup mixed berries (strawberries, blueberries, and raspberries, for example) 1/2 cup granola (use a low-sugar option) Fresh mint leaves for garnish

Instructions:

1. In a bowl, join the chia seeds, almond milk, honey or maple syrup, and

vanilla concentrate. Give everything a thorough stir to combine.

2. After about five minutes, stir the chia seed mixture once more to prevent clumping. Over the next fifteen minutes, carry out this procedure a few more times.

3. The chia seed pudding should be refrigerated for at least two hours, or until it thickens and resembles pudding.

4. Once the chia seed pudding is prepared, set up the parfait layers.

5. Layer the granola, mixed berries, and chia seed pudding in serving bowls or glasses. Ending with a sprinkle of granola on the top layer, repeat the layers until you reach the top.

6. Decorate the parfait with new mint leaves for added newness and show.

7. Serve the chia seed pudding parfait right away for a healthy and filling dessert that is good for gout.

8. Time for preparation: About 10 minutes of chilling time: 2 hours or more

Printed in Great Britain
by Amazon

37583043R00030